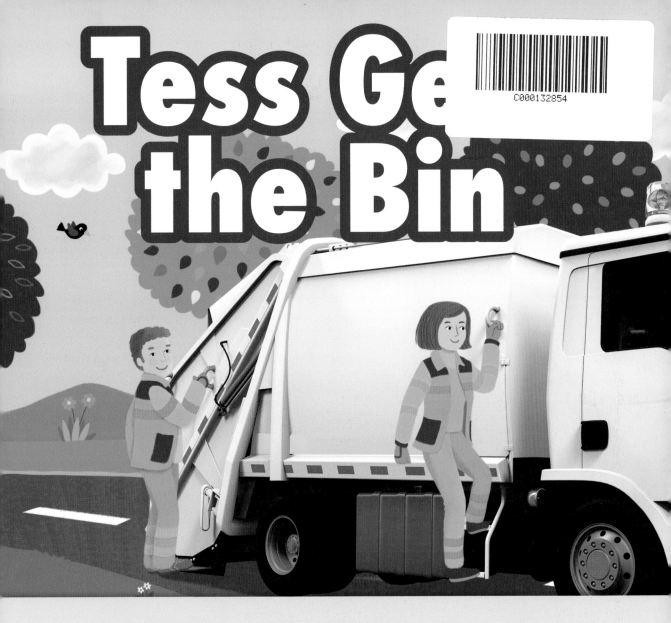

Tess Ge the Bin

Written by Sarah Loader

Illustrated by Noopur Thakur

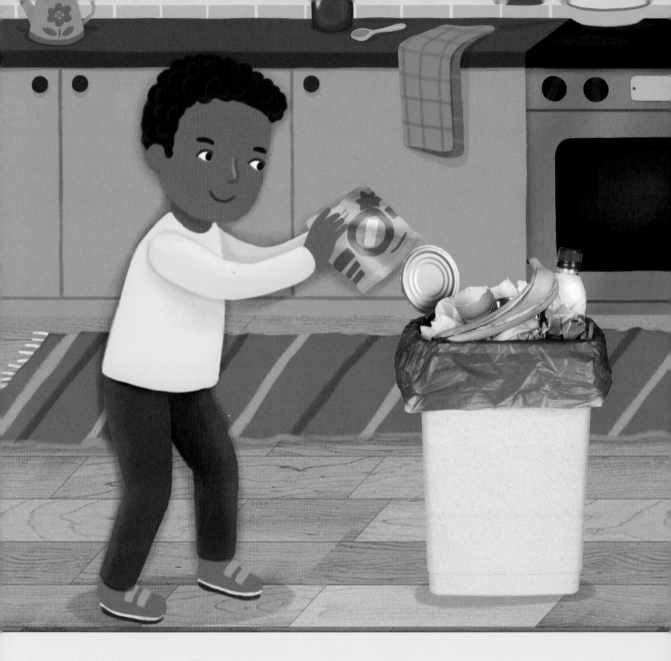

I pop it into the bin.

2

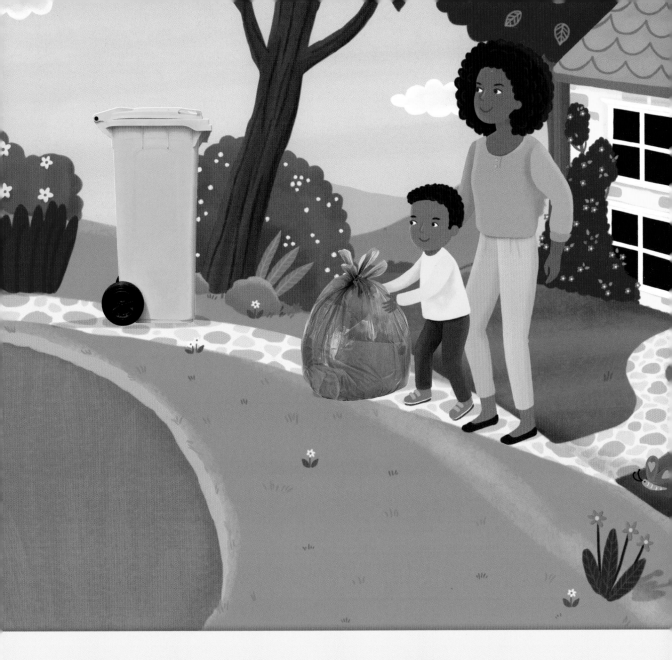

The bin is on the hilltop.

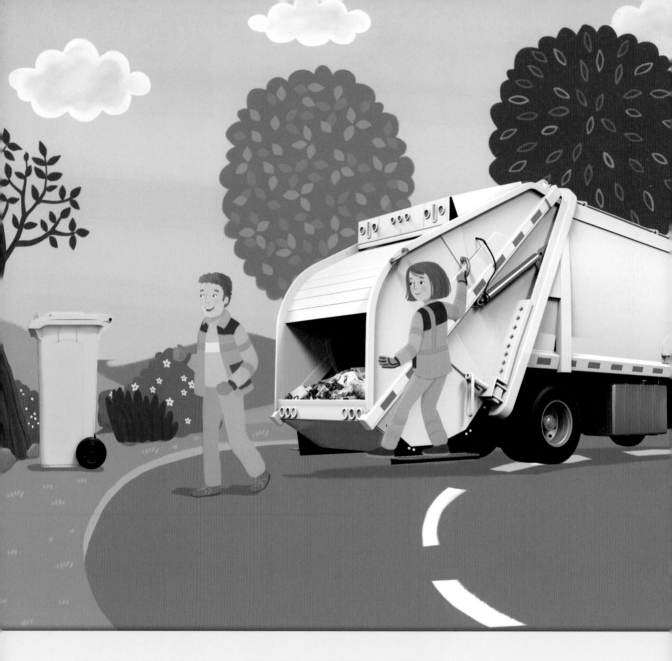

Tess and Fin get off.

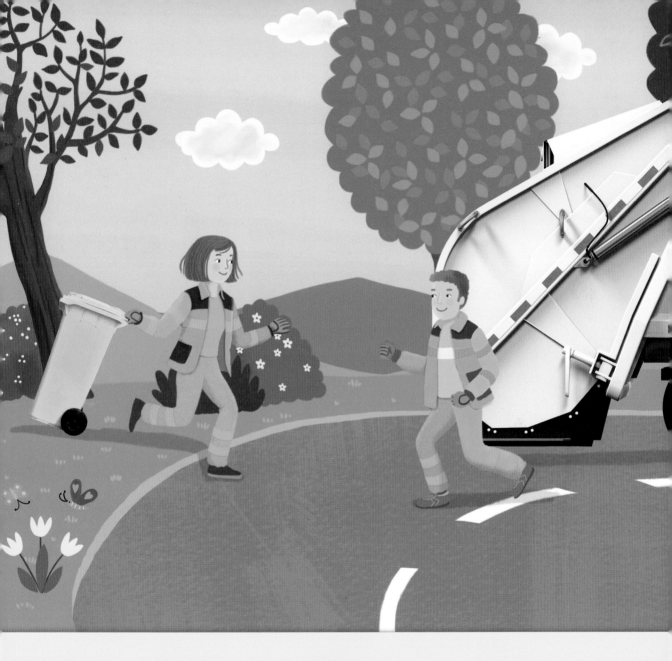

Tess picks up the bin.

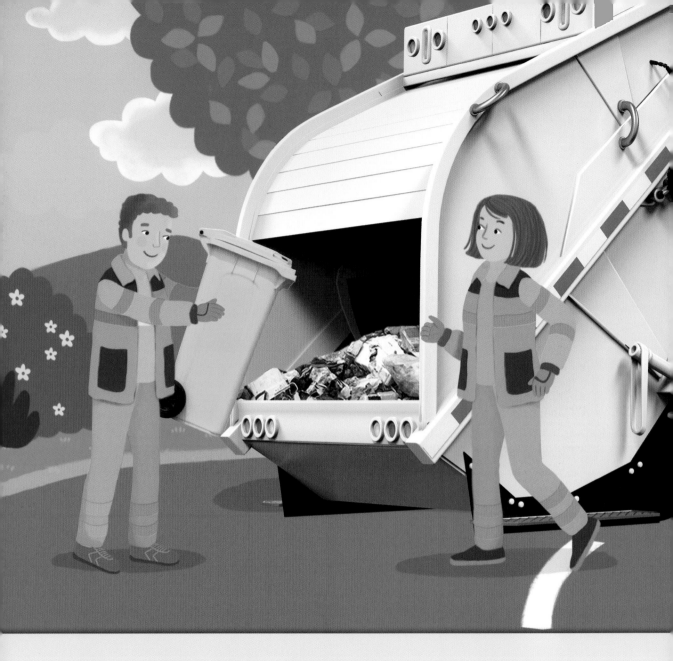

Fin lets the bin go. It tips.

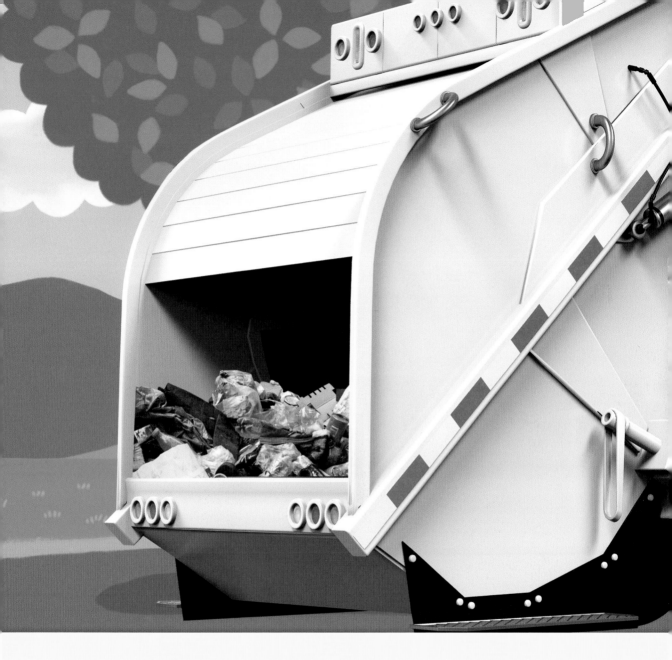

A big din and a big mess.

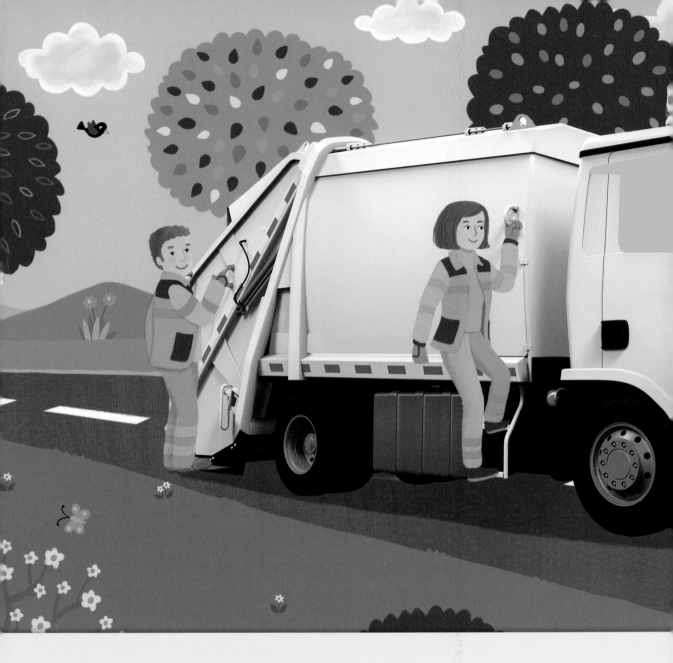

Tess and Fin get on.